Stop, take a breath, and reassess life

Fatsani Dogani, PhD

ISBN:0-994197-0-6
ISBN-13:978-0-9994197-00

DEDICATION

This book is dedicated to my amazing family for all the support they have showered me with over the years. To my husband and kids , thank you for putting up with my crazy hectic schedule. Mum and dad I will forever be grateful for the amazing job you have done in raising me to believe in my abilities and for encouraging me to follow my dreams To my brothers and sisters I love you and appreciate you daily. Finally a special dedication to my Late brother Maxwell, may you continue guiding as from above, you may be gone but you will never be forgotten.

CONTENTS

DISCLAIMER

The book is based on true facts and events, but in order to maintain personal privacy of those that I have written about I have changed the names of some of the people involved including that of my husband. Those that already know us obviously already know his real name but it was his request to me to change his name and I am honoring that. I have also opted to be vague in my reference to the different doctors we dealt with and you will also note that I do not refer to any hospital names.

1 INTRODUCTION

As an Intensive Care Unit (ICU) nurse that has worked in the ICU for the vast majority of my nursing career I generally thought I had seen it all. Caring for very sick patients and trying to be there for family members can eventually take its toll on you but it was my own personal life experience that has made me stop, take a breath and reassess life.

As of the writing of this book, my husband who is only 41 years old recently had to have spinal surgery for the removal of a spinal tumor. Going through that was and has been an experience that I find difficult to describe in simple words. Where you would expect to have a bag full of mixed emotions to explain the feelings I have had, I can only say that I have mainly tried to remain calm and collected. During what could have easily been an overwhelming point in my life I chose to always look at the brighter side of things. I realized early on that negative thinking and feeling sorry for myself was not going to get me anywhere. I chose faith and it has served me well.

To understand why this type of mindset has served me well you have to first understand where I am coming from. This book aims in most part to share that even during the darkest hours there is a higher being looking out for us. I choose to believe that God had the best intentions for us. When you read my story, you will begin to understand why I say this. I believe that the circumstances surrounding my husband's diagnosis and treatment were nothing short of a miracle. To put things into perspective, despite having had back pain for several years my husband's previous Doctor never did a thorough work up to get to the bottom of things. Don't get me wrong, he did order some diagnostics but in my opinion these were not enough. It may not be right for me to speculate but I can't help but think that his tumor could have been diagnosed a lot sooner than it was, I can't help but wonder what could have been discovered sooner had an earlier MRI been performed. A change of doctors, a back injury and a detailed workup by a doctor who I can only describe as the most brilliant doctor I have ever met resulted in the diagnosis of a spinal tumor. (All this came at a time of personal-development on my part). I think my coping was in most part influenced by the fact that I had started working on my personal improvement. A very good friend of mine introduced me to Tony Robbins several years ago. If you know Tony Robbins then you know that he is at the top of the self-improvement spectrum. Amazing how a change in mindset can change ones whole outlook on life. Tony Robbins's teachings have made me realize the power of self-responsibility, i.e. only I have the power to control how I react to my circumstances. I believe this is one reason why I have been able to cope so well with what might have previously broken me.

In writing this book it is my hope that sharing our story will help those that find themselves going through difficult situations similar to what we have gone through. What my experience has taught me is to always try and look at the brighter side of the situation and to have faith. There is truth to the saying "whatever doesn't break us can only make us stronger". I know this is easier said than done but once you start looking at the positive side of given situations you will find that this type of attitude makes coping with the difficult situations in life that much easier. I now find myself responding to challenging situations with statements such as "everything happens for a reason" and " this too shall pass". My experience showed me that I cannot always control what happens to me but I have control over how I respond to any given situation. I went from being a confident ICU nurse to being a family member of a patient reliant on the medical staff to care my husband back to health. It was a unique situation to find myself in but I knew I needed to trust in their knowledge and expertise as I expect family members of my patients to have the same trust in my expertise.

We survived the hospitalization and are now going through the recovery. I have been journaling this experience and after reading my journal my husband encouraged me to write this book. After some deep reflection and thinking I have decided to write this book to offer some words of hope and encouragement to those that might be going through similar situations. My experience has made me re-assess my life, it was the wakeup call I needed to jump start my hopes and aspirations. If anything, my husband's illness/operation made me realize that tomorrow is never promised and as such it is best to treat my time on this earth as a gift from god and to cherish each day and to use my god given gifts to my best ability. Given this new found awakening I realized that the time for living and attaining is now. I have always wanted to write a book and if my first book can offer some words of wisdom to even one person then I would have achieved something. I hope you enjoy reading this book and can find some value in it. Please also share it with those that you feel will find some value in reading it.

2 OUR STORY

Let me begin by giving some sort of background to who I am. I am a critical care nurse that has worked in the Intensive Care Unit for 15 of the 17 years I have been a nurse. I am happily married with three wonderful children. Our oldest is a 17-year-old boy who will be going off to college soon, he is followed by our 9-year-old daughter. Our last born is our genius 7-year-old son. My husband and I are originally from Malawi but we have lived in the United States for the past 11 years. I have a PhD in Public Health and I also recently established an online clothing store with my best friend from elementary school. Most people that know me think that I work too hard. I get a lot of "I don't know how you do it, kids, work, and a business". For me it really is about self-preservation, I like being busy and I feel like time not spent doing something is time wasted. That is why after graduating from nursing school I went straight through and started graduate school despite having a new baby at home and working full time as a nurse on a busy kidney transplant unit. Hard work is nothing new - it gives me a purposeful life. Don't get me wrong, I can be a bit of a procrastinator, take writing this book for instance. I have always said I wanted to write a book but never went through to actually finishing one. I have several unfinished 10 to 20 page books that I have started to write that remain saved on my laptop , so who knows, this might be the beginning of my authoring journey. I am also one person that is not scared of change. As a child growing up I had the opportunity to live in different countries and I think that is what makes me pliable to change. I like to look at change as an opportunity for growth. I feel I have a lot of life experience that makes me open minded and willing to look at the bigger picture in many given situations.

I met my husband whom I shall refer to as Tony, when I was 18 years old and I have been with him ever since, so he can be considered my high school sweet heart. I met Tony when I briefly attended college in Malawi, my country of birth. We dated for just under a year before I moved back to England to continue my nursing studies. We survived six months of a long-distance relationship before he followed suite and moved to England for his college studies. It was not easy being apart for that length of time especially in that day and age. I was 18 and madly in love. Without giving away my age, those were the days when internet was just starting and it was dialup internet that we used to use, I also had to rely on calling cards and we communicated through regular snail mail. Through it all we became closer and I couldn't have been happier when he was finally able to come and join me. We were both so young but madly in love. We had our son 3 years later and we started to make a life in England. Tony hated living in England as he always had the desire to move to the United States. He had briefly lived in San Diego during his college years and fell in love with the city. It was therefore always his desire to move back to the United States. Some years later we were able migrate to the US. We moved to the US in January of 2006 and at that time we were just a family of three. We have since made a life here in the US and have had two more children to make our family complete. We are blessed to also have my retired parents live with us. They have their home in Malawi but usually travel here and stay with us for lengths of time to help us with looking after our kids. As most people know childcare can be a challenge.

We are living the American dream and trying to build a future for our children. With that comes responsibilities and obligations. We both went back to school to pursue further studies all in the hope of creating better opportunities for our family. We are both gainfully employed but with the responsibilities of student loans and providing for our kids there is always that openness to look for other opportunities. With the financial strain and stress of student loan repayments I didn't want to play the victim card and that played a big role in pushing me to start a business which is steadily growing. My husband has also always wanted to start a business but his long commute to work meant that he was never able to find the time to spend on creating a business. There was always the thought of we will get to it with time but I have now learned that time can sneak by you, and before you know it 10 years can go by without any progress being made towards your goals. Our experience shows that there are times when things happen that are beyond your control and this can easily throw everything in disarray. As much as it can throw you for a loop I am here to share that how you deal with it is really in your control. It is that simple, you have all the power to control how you deal with all the things that happen in your life. All it requires is a decision on how you choose to deal with any given challenge. I am going to use my story to show you how easily this concept can be applied. Our family went through a very difficult time and it could have been so easy to become a victim of the situation because finding out that Tony had a spinal tumor was devastating news to deal with. We decided to go with faith and focus on the positives. We are also aware of the fact that we are fortunate to be living in the USA. My husband has been fortunate to have had access to the great healthcare, we live in the USA, I work for a hospital that offers my family great health insurance coverage. It hasn't escaped my mind that we could have easily been in a different country and the outcome could have so easily been different. Not to put anyone on blast (okay maybe the intention is there) but we could have easily been in Malawi our home country, where the healthcare system has steadily been falling apart as the years have progressed. The president himself chooses to get his healthcare here in the USA and he is not ashamed to admit this. Other notable government officials also travel outside the country for their healthcare needs. The Malawian healthcare system is broken and it needs to be fixed. I am hoping we can now start the narrative on how we can improve the healthcare system in Malawi so that the average person gets the opportunity to have basic health needs met. I plan on using my platform to bring attention to the plight of the Malawian people. I am sure those that are from Malawi will agree that we all have relatives that are somehow affected by the lack of adequate healthcare in Malawi. The fact that I am privileged to have access to healthcare services is not lost on me.

In writing this book I am sharing our experience with dealing with an unexpected health diagnosis in the hope that others can learn from our experience. I will add where relevant a list of lessons that can be learned at the end of each chapter.

3 GETTING THE NEWS

My 41-year-old husband whom I shall refer to as Tony has generally
been healthy except for a car accident he had over 20 years ago.
However, two years ago, he started complaining of some back pain. He
went to see his then doctor who ordered an x-ray and physical therapy
treatment. Tony went for the physical therapy treatment but it never
quite got rid of the nagging pain. In June of 2016 after months of me
telling him to switch to a doctor that was closer to home he finally
decided to look for a new doctor. I give him credit because he did his
due diligence in researching and selecting his current doctor, who I
consider a hero. I developed a high admiration for this doctor at our first
meeting. I had returned home from work one day after having worked
the night shift, and found my husband lying in bed in agony. When I
asked him what was wrong he said that he was in complete agony after
he had hurt his back the previous night. He had been exercising and
while lifting a 20-pound weight and he just heard a pop and felt a
shooting pain to his lower back. He then apparently dragged himself to
bed and called for our son to get him some pain medication. He was still
in a lot of pain and had called his work to let them know that he would
not be going in that day. I went into nurse mode and asked him to
describe his pain, and did a mini assessment of my own. It sounded bad
and I knew he had to see a Doctor or be taken to urgent care. I work a
long distance from home, meaning I usually get home around 0900 in

the morning so this was already around 1000 in the morning. I called his doctor's office and requested an emergency appointment. I was expecting to be given an appointment for the following week which is usually what happens at most offices. Surprisingly I was told that if I could make it there in the next 30 minutes the doctor would see us. This was a shocker if you know how doctors' offices work then you know that it's almost unheard of to get an appointment the same day. I knew I couldn't make it in half an hour but I took the appointment anyway. I had to help my husband get to the car and this took some doing because he is 6'3" and two and a half times my weight. He would never forgive me if I were to write down his actual weight. By some miracle, we made it to the car and I drove as though my life depended on it. We got to the doctor's office about 45 minutes later and had to wait a little bit to be seen. This is how special this doctor is, he shortened his lunch break to see us. Mind you this is a doctor who we had never met before it was basically our first interaction with him.

He looked at my husband and examined him briefly and knew straight away what was wrong with him. I especially loved his bedside manner, he was not condescending at all (not that most doctors are). I have made it a point not to disclose the fact that I am a nurse when I go into Doctors' offices, as I don't want them to assume I know everything. Specialization is real, nursing school was a long time ago and although I am very good at what I do I am not specialized in everything medical. I thereby rely on other people's knowledge as well. The doctor had one of those spinal dummies in his office and he explained that my husband had a disc bulge of the lower spine and what he was recommending was rest, physiotherapy, and some good meds. He even gave him 2 weeks off work which was great because Tony has a long commute to work by train. Tony went through the treatment as recommended and continued with physiotherapy for another 4-week period. He would work from home on the days that he had physical therapy.

As treatment for this was coming to an end he developed a bulge and pain in a different position of his back, this was below his shoulder blades. He went back to the Doctor and he in turn ordered different tests to help him figure out what the problem could be. First came an x-ray and then an ultrasound, the ultrasound showed something but it was not very conclusive. The x-ray on the other hand didn't really show up much. An MRI was then ordered, I knew there was something wrong when the Doctor asked for my husband to go into his office so that they could discuss the results. A phone call is usually good enough for reporting results. A face to face usually means there is something abnormal to report. Well in our situation that was exactly the case. The MRI had picked up a tumor that was in the spine between the T4 to T6 area. When I said that God works in wondrous ways I really mean it. If you recall this was a new doctor to us. Well what are the chances that my husband selected a primary care physician that just happens to have extensive experience as a radiologist and used to be a professor in Radiology Medicine. In most cases, there would be a zero chance but in our case, we were that lucky. Our doctor just happened to be the most experienced primary care physician we could ever have hoped for. He knew how to proceed and he was very reassuring, this guy was on the ball. He put all the relevant referrals in place. Although the MRI had identified that there was a tumor there was still a need to identify what type of tumor this was and this required further tests and analysis by other specialists. We were therefore referred to a neurosurgeon, an oncologist, and a radiation oncologist. This was officially the beginning of the tumor journey. Can you see the foresight of this amazing doctor? He knew based on his extensive experience what he expected the treatment plan to be so there began our journey. Based on our experience I have formulated a list of pointers to consider when choosing a primary care physician. Your primary care physician is the doctor you will visit for most of your healthcare needs, especially if you have an HMO he is the person who you will see for your routine healthcare needs as well as the one who will make the referrals to other specialists as the needs arise. The US healthcare system is complex and remains a work in progress (just look at Obama Care and the arguments for and against it). We have HMO health insurance so we mainly deal with a primary care physician thus the need to choose a primary care physician that you can be comfortable with. There are four main types of health insurance plans namely

Health Maintenance Organization (HMOs)

Preferred provider organization (PPO)

Exclusive Provider Organization (EPOs)

Point-of-service(POS) plans, and

High-deductible health plans which may be linked to health savings accounts.

It is important to research the best fit for you and your family when selecting the type of insurance plan you want but sometimes you might not have the option to choose. Take me for example, I have HMO insurance that is employer sponsored and that's how I have health coverage for my family. I am okay with this type of coverage although others do not like it because it gives you a limited choice of which physicians you can see. You basically must stick to the physicians that are within your network. This type of plan requires you to have a primary care physician who is then responsible for making the referrals for you to see a specialist in case you need to see one. That is why it is important to take the time to choose your primary care physician. Here are some pointers to consider when selecting your primary care physician.

1.Take the time to research your Doctors background and experience. This can be an important factor if you end up developing medical issues.

2. Try and select a doctor whose offices are physically close to you. There is nothing worse than having to drive a long distance to see your doctor in an emergency.

3. Select a doctor that has an excellent bedside manner. You want someone that you will feel comfortable talking to. There is nothing worse than feeling rushed when dealing with a doctor. There is usually a

valid reason as to why you go and see a doctor, you therefore want to have someone who is compassionate and understanding. Yelp now has reviews on doctors. It is in your best interest to read other patient reviews to help in your physician selection process. Be open minded when reading negative reviews especially if there is one negative review out of all positive reviews, angry patient syndrome might be a factor.

4. Ask for doctor recommendations from neighbors or friends. This is especially useful if you are new to a neighborhood.

5. Start your search by checking on your insurance companies' website. They always have a list of the doctors that accept your insurance. This is a great starting point and it also helps you save time as you will already have a list to start from.

6. It is also important to check which hospital they are affiliated with , especially if they also double up as hospitalists and also see patients in the hospital setting. You also want to know the rating of that hospital. You will most likely want to go to a hospital with a good rating.

4 TESTING AND DIAGNOSIS

To put everything into time perspective let me go back and provide a timeline of events. June 2016 was when my husband's back injury occurred, the MRI testing happened sometime in July, by August we had the referrals for the three specialists. The first appointment was with an oncologist, these are the doctors that usually deal with fighting blood disorders such as cancers. With my husband having a non-identified tumor it was expected that the oncologist would provide some sort of treatment plan.

The initial appointment with the oncologist did not result in anything much being recommended as the oncologist felt it was best to sit and wait and see what the other two specialists would recommend and the initial plan was to see him again in 3 months, this was August mind you. I respect other people's professions and I figured this was a doctor who knew what he was doing. I did wonder why a biopsy was not recommended but I figured we would wait and see what the other specialists would recommend.

Our second appointment was with a neurosurgeon, this was an older guy who has been in the game for a while. He also had the same let's sit and wait approach, his rationale kind of made some sense. He said he did not want to mess around with operating on the spine because of the high risk associated with operating on such a sensitive part of the body.

Any wrong move could easily result in paralysis or worse and since the tumor was currently not causing any obvious symptoms there was no need to rock the boat. Mind you Tony was getting regular nagging pain but apparently, this was not a significant neurological symptom. The neurosurgeon therefore also recommended a sit and wait approach where we would have a repeat MRI in three months to see whether the tumor would have grown. Having respect for his opinion we listened and waited to see the next specialist.

We saw the radiology oncologist a week after seeing the neurosurgeon, I was sure to ask about doing a biopsy since we didn't know what type of tumor we were dealing with but he felt it was also best to wait the three months as the tumor wasn't causing any symptoms though he did recommend a PET scan which would be able to pick up whether the tumor was cancerous or not. A positron emission tomography (PET) scan is a type of imaging test that uses a radioactive substance to show how organs and tissues are working.

In hindsight, we probably should have been more assertive and asked for more to be done but at that time we were respecting these doctor's recommendations as they were the specialists in their fields and supposedly knew what they were doing.

We went back to our primary care physician about a week later for a routine follow up and he was shocked that nothing had been done by the specialists he had referred Tony to. At this checkup, it was discovered that Tony had very high blood pressure, he prescribed blood pressure medication for him and asked him to come back after a week to see the nurse just for a blood pressure check. He wanted to give the medications a week , the follow up appointment was for him to be able to assess how well the medication was working. We were also advised to buy a blood pressure monitor and to get into the habit of observing Tony's blood pressure closely. As I mentioned previously this doctor has been our best advocate and I wish every doctor was like him. You will understand why I have such deep-rooted admiration and respect for him as you learn about what he has done for my husband and how he has gone above and beyond the call of duty. We went home and Tony started on the blood pressure medication and we continued with life as normal while waiting for these follow up doctors' appointments that were scheduled for some time in November. A week went by and Tony went in for his blood pressure checkup appointment what went down from there you might want to sit down for. My husband went in for his appointment with the nurse, they checked his blood pressure and surprisingly or not so surprisingly it was extremely high. The medication was supposed to bring the blood pressure down but it hadn't made a bit of a difference to the numbers. The nurse reported the findings to the doctor and he was not happy with the situation. He went and did a detailed neurological exam on my husband and he picked up on some neurological deficits that Tony was exhibiting. His right side was weaker than the left side and the high blood pressure was an indication that he was now officially symptomatic.

I was not there but per Tony my hero doctor was on a war path, fighting on his behalf. He called the oncologist to express his frustration at the situation and to give him a piece of his mind. In his opinion the specialist doctors had dropped the ball by taking a sit and wait approach. I have since spoken to him and this is where he says he was coming from. He felt that the specialists had basically dropped the ball, here was an essentially healthy 40-year-old guy with a spinal tumor and nobody had done anything about it, to him sitting and waiting was considered not doing anything. Tony was 40 at the time all this was happening. Hero doctor was perplexed by the fact that they were all taking a sit and wait attitude. He was a doctor with experience in this type of thing as he had worked for years in a teaching hospital on the east coast. He felt the doctors in California did not practice medicine with the same type of urgency. He had essentially handed them the diagnosis and the reason he had referred us to the three specialists was because he was expecting them to do something about the tumor. Now here we were weeks later, nothing had been done yet this young guy was now experiencing symptoms.

He got on the phone with the medical oncologist's office demanding to speak to the doctor, apparently the nurses were playing buffer and would not let the doctor come to the phone. My husband did hear parts of the conversation and from the sounds of things my hero doctor really went above and beyond in advocating for his treatment. He expressed his frustrations with how my husband's case had been handled and he was disappointed that nothing tangible had been done. He told him that there was no way he was going to send my husband home with the blood pressure as high as it was. In other words the time for sitting and waiting was over. As he explained to us later these types of tumors have been known to burst and that was his fear. My husband was apparently having neurogenic hypertension because of the tumor and the fact that he was also experiencing added symptoms was not a good sign. After a very long heated discussion between our hero doctor and the oncologist it was decided that Tony should go to the oncology medical offices to receive some urgent medical treatment. The tumor was obviously misbehaving, and the thought process was that it was causing swelling within the spine which was now affecting the blood supply through the spine and thus resulting in the high blood pressure and the weakness and numbness on the right side. Tony then drove from our hero doctor's office to the medical oncologist office where he received an intravenous drip of dexamethasone, a steroid that works to help with reducing swelling. The purpose was to reduce the swelling that had developed within the spine from the tumor. After his drip, he was told to go to the emergency room to have further follow up testing.

While all this was going on, I was at home sleeping after having worked the night before and I was scheduled to go back to work that night as well. I woke up to find multiple missed calls from Tony. I usually put my phone on silence to ensure I get adequate sleep. Seeing the multiple missed calls, I knew something must be up. I called him back and he told me that he was at the hospital. You can imagine my shock, I had gone to bed knowing that he was going to see the nurse to have his blood pressure checked. Once he explained what was going on I knew I had to think fast on my feet. He tried to reassure me by saying he was just there for some tests but I told him I would drive there as soon as I could call work and tell them I wasn't coming in. I called the charge nurse and literally had a mini mental break down, the reality of the situation hit me in that instant. I apologized for cancelling my shift and briefly explained that my husband was in a hospital emergency room getting different tests done and I had to be there with him. I had no idea what the plan was going to be but I just knew that I had to be there. The charge nurse was very understanding and supportive and told me not to worry but to do what was best for me and my family. I had no way of knowing that I would not return to work for a while yet.

The lessons I can share from this aspect of our experience is the need to become your own advocate when it comes to seeking medical care. You cannot always afford to take the sit and wait approach. There are certain situations where your voice has to become loud, this is where educating yourself on your illness comes in handy. Here are some key takeaways that can help you as you deal with new diagnosis and treatment plans.

1. Ask questions and make notes when you are first told about a new diagnosis. It is difficult to retain information in high stress situations and receiving a scary diagnosis is one of those high stress situations. Although you might think you are understanding what is being said in the moment , your recall of the information might not be so great.
2. Take the time to research the condition and recommended treatment plans. Try and become an expert on your condition so that you can get an understanding of what to expect and be prepared for it.
3. Get an understanding of the rationale behind your doctor's recommended treatment plan. Ask questions about all the different treatment options that are available to you. Therefore, having some knowledge about your condition will come in handy you in case you have to ask the Doctor why he chooses one treatment plan over another. I know we might all suffer from googlelitis but I encourage google only for informative

purposes, keep an open mind about what you read on the internet.

4. Research the specialists that you will need to work with so you get an understanding of what they do and what others say about them.
5. Become your own advocate by following up on tests and results. Learn when tests results are due back and do the necessary chasing up if needed.
6. Keep communicating with your primary care physician because we have learned that not all specialists are good at informing your PCP about what is going on.

5 THE HOSPITALIZATION

After calling off at work I called Tony back to let him know that I was going to drive down to the hospital to be there with him. At this point we did not know what the treatment plan was going to be. Being a typical man, all he could complain about was the fact that he was hungry and wanted me to bring him something to eat, I assured him that I would stop somewhere to get him something to eat. I was still a bit tearful but I collected myself and went to break the news to my parents who are our in-house babysitters. When I say God works in wondrous ways, I use my parents as another example of gods faithfulness. By God's grace, I was able to leave my kids to go be with my husband with the full knowledge that they would be okay under the care of my parents. When I left my house that day I did not know that it would be two days before I would be back. I left thinking that I was going to be with Tony as he underwent some tests and then we would come back home while they worked on a treatment plan. All I could tell my parents was that I was not going to work that night but was instead driving to the hospital that Tony was at so I could be there with him. I said goodbye to the kids, who took it well. I have relatively independent kids. I have worked nights for years and they are used to seeing me leave the house to go to work. They wondered why I wasn't in my scrubs, I explained to them that I was going to the hospital to keep Dad company because he was getting his back examined. Since Tony had been on an off from work with his initial back injury they didn't find anything shocking about this. My parents, supportive as always told me not to worry about anything as they would have the home front handled.

I therefore left home knowing that the kids would be well looked after. I passed by In and Out Burger to buy some food but when I got to the hospital around 6 pm I was told that Tony was not allowed to eat. The oncologist had apparently had a discussion with the neurosurgeon who suggested that he come to the hospital for further work up. It appears this tumor was not behaving as expected and they had to figure out what to do with it. Remember how I said the first neurosurgeon that Tony saw had been in the game a bit too long, well his partner was younger than him and more technologically savvy. Well as our luck would have it the younger surgeon was the one that was on call and he is the one that handled my husband's case that day. I arrived at the hospital around 6pm. I was starving and as mean as it was I ate my burger in front of Tony who now was hooked up to the monitor getting his blood pressure frequently checked as it was still very high. He had been given a room in the emergency room while waiting for his tests to be completed. The main test that he was really waiting on was an MRI.

It was very tough for me to sit there and watch and not do anything about the alarm that kept going off every time his blood pressure was getting read. A combination of the tumor and pain was causing the blood pressure to stay consistently high. I didn't want to self-identify as a nurse so I did not mention to anyone that I was a nurse. I know from experience some nurses can feel like they are being second guessed and I didn't want to come across as a know it all and ask too many questions. The nurses were great they kept us informed of what was going on the whole time. We were told that Tony would have to be admitted that night and that the neurosurgeon would come see us later that night. I knew then that I would not be going home that night. I was thankful for the changes that have recently taken place in healthcare, most hospitals now allow family members to stay overnight as a care partner. Tony went for his MRI and then transferred to the orthopedic floor. Since the surgeon hadn't yet seen him he still couldn't eat. Once in the room we decided to make the most of it, we were in a modern relatively new hospital that had rooms with a pull-out chair for family members to sleep on. We decided to pretend we had gone away for a romantic getaway. We chatted and watched some TV while waiting for the surgeon to come explain what the plan of action was going to be. The admitting hospitalist came to see us and officially admitted my husband. He had apparently spoken to the surgeon who had told him that he would be in to see us and that Tony could eat anything for the time being but he would not be allowed to eat or drink anything after midnight. It was just as well I had kept the In and Out Burger, the nurses graciously warmed it up for us and Tony was finally able to eat something that day, what a treat.

The neurosurgeon finally made it to see us at around 11pm that night. I will summarize the conversation as briefly as possible without putting in too much jargon. I liked the surgeon because he had an excellent bedside manner. He was friendly and very well spoken; if you are a nurse then you might have had to deal with some surgeons that can be arrogant and condescending but not in this case. This neurosurgeon took the time to talk to us and he made sure we felt free to ask him questions. The core of the situation was that Tony had this tumor that had now become symptomatic, since it had not been biopsied he could only speculate on the type of tumor that it could be. He explained that based on his experience spinal tumors are usually one of three main types, he would only be able to tell what type of tumor it could be during surgery. He explained that if he went ahead with surgery there were 3 possible outcome scenarios depending on the type of tumor it could be

Tumor type 1= best case scenario, this type of tumor would have a clear border that would be easy to remove surgically meaning short surgery and end of the problem

Tumor type 2= this type of tumor would not have a clear demarcation that would make it difficult to remove without causing major spinal damage. If this was the type of tumor he would simply take a biopsy and close him up and we would have to figure out a different treatment plan, possibly chemotherapy or radiation

Tumor type 3= also not amenable to surgery he would also have to take a biopsy and figure out different treatment plan.

Given this explanation plus the risks associated with any type of spinal surgery which are scary as they include possibility of paralysis and death he asked us how we wanted to proceed. The other option was to sit and wait, but we know where that had gotten us. The possible risks were scary indeed and I have never seen my husband be more decisive than he was in that instant. He wanted to proceed with the surgery because he was tired of not knowing what type of tumor it was. Per Tony the stress of not knowing was worse than the risks that had been described. He was willing to take the chance so he could get some peace and closure from this never-ending agony. Just like that the major decision of having spinal surgery for the removal of a spinal tumor was made. Once all our questions had been answered we were at peace with the decision to have the surgery. He was going to schedule the surgery for the following morning and he left us to digest the news while he went to make the necessary arrangements. Since he was a technologically savvy surgeon we were reassured by the fact that he works very closely with a company that has equipment that would monitor my husband's nerve function throughout the surgery to ensure that they were keeping a close eye on his nerve function.

It might sound strange to hear but my husband coped well with the news of an impending surgery. He is well loved by a lot of people and I knew we had to somehow share the news. I drafted a simple note to text to friends and family and it went like

Hello so and so, hope you are well, just to let you know after Tony's recent back injury, he has continued to have pain, they found a lump on MRI that they want to test. So we are now at ----- hospital, he is going

for surgery at 0830 to have a sample taken. Keep him in your prayers

We had never been in a position like this before so we did not know how to handle the breaking the news aspect of this whole ordeal. We were not in the mood to answer questions because there was a lot for us to take in as well, that is why we went with text. Being in the medical field I knew that surgery came with its own risks and I don't know how I would have responded if I had been the one that needed surgery. I had to respect my husband's decision because he was the one that had to deal with the pain and the fear of the unknown. I can only imagine what knowing that you have a tumor in your spine can do to a person. There were the few that texted back and I appreciated their best wishes. It's always a good feeling to know that there are people out there that look out for us

Being that I am a nurse in the ICU I feel like I have seen so much, I had to ask Tony what his wishes regarding medical care were. It's funny how as a nurse I encourage my patients and their loved ones to address this aspect of their healthcare wishes and I had yet to sit down and really talk to my spouse about it. In case most of you are wondering what I am rambling about I will briefly explain. Most times when you are admitted into the hospital the medical team is obligated to ask whether you have an advanced directive. This document covers certain aspects about your care, for instance if something happened to the point where you are unable to make medical decisions for yourself who would you want as your surrogate decision maker. If your heart stopped would you want everything done to revive you. Its not as simple as I am making it out to be but it is just one of those things people don't tend to talk about in everyday conversations. Up until this point in our relationship we hadn't really had this discussion or prepared any documents to this effect. The discussion itself was not as difficult as you would think, Tony is very strong in his faith and he believes that God will take him when it is time but given the situation, he would want everything that could medically be done to be done for him. I felt comfortable with the discussion we had and felt I could advocate freely for him with the knowledge of what he would want done given a medical emergency. Once this heavy discussion was out of the way we relaxed and just spent some quality time together. I had already updated my parents on the plan of action and I knew they had the home situation handled.

We were in good spirits because we both felt that surgery was the best option. The quickness with which Tony had agreed to have surgery despite the associated risks was reason enough for me to be supportive of his decision. We also decided to put everything in God's hands. This is when I realized I had grown in my faith. I decided to focus on what was positive about the situation at hand. The old me would have probably been focusing on the possible risks and worry myself to death, but the new me has a much better outlook on life. I am an avid fan of Tony Robbins and one quote of his that sticks to my mind is "where focus goes energy flows". To me this means the more I focus on something the more my energy is affected by it. I chose to look at the positive aspect of the situation. There are those that might not see anything positive about our given situation but here is where I was at. I am a firm believer that everything happens for a reason. I looked at everything that had happened to Tony since his initial back injury and I decided it was God's way of looking out for us. Bear with me here, he had been going to his previous doctor for nearly two years complaining of back pain and he never once ordered anything more than a back x-ray. Here we were facing a spinal tumor just months after switching to a new doctor, if you don't see that as God looking out for us then I don't know what to call it. The reason I say this is we could have easily continued with life not knowing he had a spinal tumor and only God knows what the potential outcomes of that could have been. We at least now knew what we were dealing with and we had a plan for addressing it. We knew that by the end of the surgery we would at least have more answers to all our questions.

We prayed and put everything in God's hands and tried to get some sleep. I managed to get some sleeping hours in because I was tired, but before sleeping I had to help Tony with the preparation bath. To prevent surgical site infections hospitals require you to have a pre-operative scrub using antibacterial wipes the night before and the morning of the surgery. Tony's sleep was disturbed as the nursing staff had to keep a close eye on his blood pressure, which meant they were coming into our room every couple of hours to check on his blood pressure. Contrary to popular belief hospitals are not the best places to get rest. There is usually something going on, whether it be the nurses checking in on you, or the lab technicians getting your blood , you can certainly rely on some ongoing activity .I suppose it is at this point that it would be helpful to include some pointers on how to prepare for hospitalization and surgery as well as the dreaded talk about your living will/ healthcare wishes/advanced directive.

1. It is important to discuss what your healthcare wishes are so that your loved one has a clear understanding about what you would like done in certain medical situations. This is important in times when you are unable to make your own decisions. Having a loved one in hospital can be stressful and the added stress can come from the second guessing that might occur when your loved one has to make medical decisions for you without really knowing what you would want done in given medical situations.

2. Having this conversation is the first step in letting your loved one know what your wishes are regarding end of life care as well. There is a misconception about what this all entails that is why it is important to start having the conversation now. We are not invisible anything can happen at any given time. There is a lot of education that needs to happen on this as most people think that if they say they do not want to be resuscitated the medical staff will stop treating them which is far from the truth.

3. It is important to imagine all the worst-case scenarios and think about the quality of life you would want. Would you be ok with being dependent on life support in a nursing home, and if so for how long?

4. If you are a couple start to plan and consider how you would handle the hospitalization of your significant other, we didn't

have this figured out because we never expected that one of us would get hospitalized. We have since learned the value of planning.

5. If you have kids start to think about how you would handle their care in case one of you was hospitalized. Have plans in place and talk to your friends about their willingness to help in as needed cases in case of any medical emergencies.

6. Consider whether you would be able to financially survive any specific length of hospitalization. We tend to live in the present and don't plan for the unexpected eventualities, I now fully understand why there is such an emphasis on having an emergency fund . I discuss a bit more on finances in a later chapter.

6 THE SURGERY

The day of the surgery was here, we were wheeled to the operating room by the transporters. We were met by our pre-operative nurse and she was very nice and attentive. She went over the consent form and she explained what to expect. Then the surgeon came to see us, he went over his plan and I had some questions for him regarding the after care, amazing what a night of sleep can do for the brain. He told us that Tony would be admitted to the ICU for closer monitoring after the surgery. He explained that the length of the surgery would be determined by the type of tumor they found. We were both reassured by this surgeon, like I said his bedside manner was amazing and he was very knowledgeable. I was also reassured by the fact that he was going to be working closely with a team that would be monitoring my husband's nerve throughout the operation. Having this surgeon being on call and available to do the surgery to me was another sign that God was for us. Remember the initial surgeon had said it was too risky and it was best to sit and wait. Well here was a highly technologically savvy surgeon available for us and willing to explain everything in detail. I had a sense of peace over me because I trusted that God had brought us the most qualified person to perform the surgery. The anesthesiologist also saw us in the pre-operative suite and he went over his plan and answered all our questions to our satisfaction. It was now time for Tony to go for his surgery, we prayed together and I gave him a very big hug and kiss and went to wait for the surgery to be over.

Waiting for something is never easy so I tried to keep myself busy, I went back to our room to collect our stuff because we wouldn't be returning to that floor as he was going to go to the ICU for his recovery. I collected the bag of things that I had and decided to go to a friend's house to get showered and refreshed. I couldn't relax because I wanted to make sure I would be there after the surgery so that I could get updated about how the surgery went. Since he had said the surgery could last anywhere between 3 to 5 hours I wanted to be there for the 3-hour mark. I also had friends who said they were planning on visiting, trying to dissuade them did not work. They drove to the hospital while I was still at my friends getting showered. The reason I didn't go home to shower is because we live far from the hospital and I didn't want to take the risk of being too far away from the hospital. I drove back to the hospital to sit with our friends while we waited. I also had to call work to let them know I would not be going into work as I was scheduled to work that night. I also knew that I would have to be off from work to be available for my husband and family so it was prudent for me to call my manager and let her know that I would be requiring extended leave. This again was another sign that God was looking out for us. We live in California and although people complain about how expensive California is, I am grateful I work in this wonderful state. I am eligible to take time off to care for a spouse, child, or parent and the state ensures that my employer keeps my job. I know that if we were in a different state I would have had other stressors to contend with at a time when we both couldn't work. I talked to my manager and she was very supportive and reassured me not to worry about work. I was scheduled to be at work that weekend. Another saving grace was the fact that my parents were holding down the fort by taking over on the home front.

I went back to the hospital around 1 pm and our friends were there to keep me company while we waited for surgery to end. I appreciated the fact that the waiting area had a screen that showed the different surgeons and the case start times to keep family members updated without us having to keep asking at the reception desk. They ensured that privacy was maintained by not including the patient's names on the update board. The wait started to get unbearable but I kept positive by telling myself that a long surgery meant that the tumor was being removed. Our friends left before the surgery was over because they had to go and pick up their kids from school. I had sent a message to my mother in law the night before and she was waiting to be updated. I decided to call her before the surgery was over due to the time difference and me not wanting her to stay up anxiously waiting. My mother in law at this time was living in Malawi, thus my concern with the time difference and her having to stay up waiting to get updated. I called her and explained what the surgeon had said and told her that I felt very reassured by the surgeon and I felt that Tony was in the best possible hands. She told me she was glad I was there and she was reassured that I had a medical background. It was a big deal for her as well her first-born child was miles away undergoing surgery and I know she wanted to be here with us. Talking to her also made me feel better as reassuring her also went a long way towards reassuring me.

Three o'clock turned into four o'clock and I was now beginning to worry. I continued to say my silent prayers and eventually the surgeon emerged just before 5pm. He came and sat down to explain the outcome of the surgery. He had removed most of the tumor but since there was no clear demarcation between the tumor and the spine there were parts of the tumor that remained within the spine. He had taken samples and we would find out the pathology of the sample after three to five business days. The relief I felt was palpable, once the surgeon left the nurse came over to let me know that they were getting Tony ready to go to ICU but it might take a while. She told me to hang around the waiting area and that she would let me know which room to go to once they had transferred him to the ICU. By this time the news of the surgery and hospital admission had spread like wildfire, friends wanted to know how the surgery went and they also wanted to know how Tony was doing. I was finally notified of the room number and I went up to the 7th floor. I had to wait outside the ICU while they settled him in.

When I finally got the chance to go in to see him I was glad to see he was not intubated with multiple drips attached. I was so thankful to God for a successful operation. He was attached to the monitor as they needed to keep a very strict eye on his blood pressure. The wires and lines were not scary to me because I was familiar with them. It was good to hear his voice but I could tell he was a bit out of it because he kept repeating himself.

His friends started showing up but we had to adhere to a strict visiting schedule and the unit has a strict no visiting policy during report time which is between the hours of 7pm to 8pm. Since he was out of it I visited in the waiting area with the friends that had come to see him. Having a community of friends is amazing in times of need they kept me company and most importantly they brought me food. I had not been home and they kept me from worrying. There was a village in that waiting room and I was thankful. They took turns visiting until the nurse had to put a stop to it. Being the kind, wonderful person he is, Tony was trying to entertain his visitors and this in turn was causing his blood pressure to rise. The nurse decided that the visitors were not helping the situation even though they meant well. She asked me to stop allowing more people in to see him. I felt bad because I know they wanted to be there to give him love and support but at the same time I knew that he needed the rest. A few were understandably disappointed but they got it. When they finally all left, I went back in to the room. The blood pressure was now better controlled as he had had to be started on a medication drip to help maintain the blood pressure at the prescribed level that the surgeon wanted it to be. Tony wasn't as loopy as he had been earlier but he was sleepy and so I was. Since he was in the ICU I knew he was in excellent care as the nurse was there to make sure his blood pressure was within the range the doctor wanted it to be, the pain was under control and his neurological status remained stable. In other words, we were in for a long night of frequent monitoring. I got my pull-out chair organized and I was ready to hit the sack. I was so relieved that the operation had gone smoothly and that Tony was talking appropriately and all limbs seemed to be working well. Being the nurse that I am I had done my own neurological assessment on him. I was finally able to report to his mum that all had gone well.

Despite being in the hospital and sleeping on a pull-out chair I managed to sleep well. The next morning another good friend brought me breakfast on her way to work, I am so thankful for good friends they are there for you in your time of need and this was a time of need. We had the morning to ourselves as this was the time to get rest before the visitors started in again. The physical therapists came and they were going to attempt to try and get him sitting. I was surprised that they had orders to get him up but I suppose the surgeon was confident in his handiwork. I thought that he would have to be on bedrest for a while. They tried to get him up but based on his pain and being so soon after the surgery they decided to use the bed to sit him into a chair position instead. He looked so much better than the day before and I was once again very grateful at how well the surgery had gone. We called the kids and they were so excited to get to talk to their dad. In case you are wondering what we said to the kids about the surgery. We kept it simple, we told them that dad was staying in the hospital because he had to have surgery on his back and he would have to be in the hospital for a while. One of our friends came in to keep Tony company so that I could go and get freshened up at the same friend house I had gone to the day before. In case you are wondering about clothes, I was borrowing friends clothes and every girl usually has a brand new set of underwear hanging out somewhere.

We got a lot of visitors with it being a Saturday, since we hadn't said much about what had been going on until the group text we had sent the night before the surgery a lot of our friends were in shock about the tumor. Tony was only 40 and our friends are also that age, that is young and the thought of a tumor and possible cancer was shocking. Our story telling got better with each friend that came to visit, they all wanted to know what the deal was. Everyone wanted to know what the biopsy showed but it was too soon to know the results. We were seen by the surgeon who once again went over what he had done in the surgery and he also did a full-strength assessment to see if there was a change in Tony's strength. There was some obvious improvement and we were all very pleased by that.

Throughout that Saturday we got a steady flow of visitors including our kids and my parents. One of our close friends was kind enough to pick them up and bring them over to the hospital to come see their dad. The kids were excited to see their dad and our youngest was slightly in shock but soon settled into his usual smiling self. They bought him a card and Tony was very touched by the sentiment. Our oldest wrote a touching message letting his dad know that he wished him a quick recovery and that he was going to be a good boy and great big brother. We prayed together as a family and there was overall general sense of relief that daddy was going to be alright.

One visitor we were very grateful to receive was our pastor from our church. He drove all the way down on his Saturday to see Tony and to lead us in prayer. This again was a sign for me that god had his protective arms around us. We prayed for healing and strength and visited with him for a short while

Visitors came and went until official end of visiting which was 10pm, it would be an understatement to say that we were not exhausted by the end of it all. I hit the pillow and I was out. This was my mind and body giving into the exhaustion but it was also my mind letting go of any fears and knowing that we were over the worst. I felt that the worst was over and we now had treatment possibilities, knowing the type of tumor Tony had would only be the first step towards knowing what the best course of action should be. I once again decided to choose positivity, the way I saw it stressing over a possible what if wasn't going to get me anywhere so between the two of us we decided to focus on the now. That meant being pleased that the operation had gone well and what we now had to focus on was getting Tony back home.

Most surgeries are planned but others can happen in an emergency the advice I provide can be used for both situations especially for the person going to be waiting for the patient.

1. Plan to be there if you can, the surgeons do a good job at explaining what they are going to do and they also take the time to come out and talk to you when the surgery is done. You want to get that instant feedback from the surgeon as it does give you a sense of relief.
2. Bring some work or a book to read for the waiting period to distract yourself from overthinking. I know in this smart phone era most people would probably just have their phone and be glued on that screen. The great thing is that most hospitals now have Wi-Fi.
3. If you have kids make the necessary arrangements to minimize disrupting their schedules as much as possible. Make alternative arrangements for their care by reaching out to family or friends. This is why it is important to make an effort to make friends with other moms and dads at the kids schools.
4. Always have those emergency contacts handy in case you do have to go into the hospital for an unplanned procedure. It is therefore important to take careful consideration of who you chose to be the emergency contact for your kids at school as these are the people you will most probably have to lean on for help in difficult situations.
5. Make sure they are willing to be your emergency contacts and have a deep conversation with your designated surrogates to ensure they are actually comfortable with being the emergency contacts for your kids

7 THE RECOVERY PROCESS

The following day was a Sunday and after the excitement of all the visitors of the day before we wanted to take it easy. We were excited to hear that we were going to be transferred to a step-down unit. This was exciting because the unit had a more flexible visitor's policy than the ICU. We were transferred in the morning and this was a good thing because once again a steady stream of visitors came to see Tony. This was a big day because he could sit on the edge of the bed and stand up. Post-surgery pain was a factor that we had to deal with and the nurses were very good at trying to keep on top of it. With all the visitors' Tony was getting I decided to take advantage and decided to drive home to get some more clothes and to check up on the kids and ensure they had food supplies and everything else they might need. I needn't have worried because my parents had the whole home situation well handled. The kids were doing well and mum told me not to be stressing myself out worrying about the kids because they were all doing just fine. It was another night spent in the hospital and I was getting used to the pull-out sofas.

In all this time, I was scheduled to be working but my manager told me not to worry and to follow up with her on the Monday. In getting the house in order I called my manager on the Monday and she referred me to HR, they were going to process my leave of absence but I would need medical certification. My plan was to drive to Tony's primary care physician to get the initial paperwork signed. With trying to sort out home situation and other matters that needed my attention I was not in the room when the surgeon rounded on Tony. I got the second-hand information which he got wrong himself. Per Tony we were going to be going to another facility for him to start working on rehabilitation before being discharged home. It was his understanding that we would be returning to our room after his rehab session. The reality of it though was that we were being fully transferred to a different facility for inpatient rehabilitation services. The expectation was that we would be there for at least ten days. Transport came to pick him up at 8pm and I drove myself there. The rehab was in an older hospital and the rooms were very small, I was given a different type of pull out chair that was not as comfortable as the ones I had at the newer hospital but I had to make it work. The staff on the rehab unit were very caring they made us feel very welcome. I was surprised they let me stay the night since it was such a smaller room but I guess healthcare has really changed. I know Tony was very pleased to have me there with him the whole time. I wanted to go home just for one night of sound sleep in my own bed but the reaction I got to that from Tony showed me just how scared he was and how reliant he was on me being in the hospital with him. I therefore put that thought to the side and made peace with the fact that I would have to stay over every night until he got discharged home. The goal of rehab was to get Tony functioning as close to his baseline as was possible.

Tuesday was the initial assessment and it went well, they told us they usually do a ten day treatment plan. They worked with him in the morning and he had more sessions in the afternoon. I had to go for an appointment for myself that afternoon so I guess that worked out. A week before Tony's escalation I had a traumatic event happen to me at work that had shaken me to the core. I had avoided dealing with it because of everything else that was now going on with my family. In all the years, I have been a nurse I have never used the employee assistance service but the event had been so traumatic that I had decided to sign up for a session. I would highly recommend this service to anyone who is going through different issues and just needs a listening ear. I was so glad I had kept the appointment because I felt I needed an outlet to talk through all that had happened. Even though I had chosen to be positive about the whole process I knew enough to know that I also needed to look after me. I needed someone to talk to. I drove to my session and that is where I had my long awaited controlled breakdown. With having to talk through what had happened at work and now what happened to Tony there was a lot to deal with. I could talk through my feelings and I left the session with some coping tools. The counselor emphasized the need for self-care, she emphasized that I needed to make sure I was looking after myself as well because it seemed I had a full plate to deal with. After all, my hubby had just gone through major surgery, I had a work incident that I had to deal with plus all the logistics of ensuring the kids were dealing and keeping everyone including myself from going into full blown panic mode. I therefore tried to ensure that I was looking after myself. Sleeping at the hospital might not be considered the best form of self-care but I tried to make it work as best as I could. Months before all this happened my girlfriends from work and I had purchased tickets to watch The Lion King and it fell on day 2 of rehab. Mixed feelings aside I opted to go and watch the Broadway show with my girlfriends. I recognized that I had to do something normal, I had been in the hospital for days living on cafeteria food and the occasional homecooked meals that our friends would bring in to us. I decided to be selfish and do something for my emotional health. I got picked up and went to watch The Lion King. In case you are wondering Tony was also supportive of this. He had some physical therapy and occupational therapy sessions scheduled for that afternoon.

Going out with friends and watching The Lion King was great, I could talk to my nurse friends about my experience and this helped me out a lot. I mean this was major surgery that my husband just had. You talk about in sickness and in health during the vow section of the wedding ceremony but you never really expect to have to deal with it to that extent. Through it all I still focused on the positive aspect of the whole situation.

Even though it does suck that we went through this I remain grateful for all that went well. For starters, they found the tumor and they could do something about it, secondly, we were under the care of a great team of doctors and nurses, and thirdly we had my parents looking after our kids which was another blessing. Although I have gone a bit off tangent the point I am trying to make is that you should somehow create time for your self-care. It can be so easy to forget your own needs because you are focusing on the needs of others. I knew that I would be no use to anyone as an emotional stressed out wreck so I opted to look after me , and I am glad I took that time and went out.

The rehabilitation experience was great, we had an amazing team of nurses, therapists, social worker, and doctor and they made our stay bearable. Their attitude was amazing more so because they deal with so many different patients each with their own conditions to overcome. It is amazing how the human body can forget things we take for granted. Hubby had to literally re-learn how to get out of bed and with the pain it took a lot out of him. Due to the nature of his surgery he had to avoid twisting, he had to think through each movement he would make, from turning on his side to sitting up in bed to getting out and into the chair. He even had to follow special instructions on how to put on his socks without twisting or bending his back. Our concern was how he would handle going up and down the stairs at home. We had already started making plans to move downstairs so that he didn't have to worry about the stairs. I soon learned that the goal of rehab was to get Tony as close to functioning at his pre-operative level as possible. They were going to make sure that he could climb up and down the stairs as well as do all the other things he would normally do at home. They prepped him with getting in and out of the shower and they showed him how to handle any cooking chores without bending or twisting his back. He progressed through rehab quickly. We were given a discharge goal of Friday so instead of being in rehab for the ten days we were only there for four days. We were happy to be going back home there is nothing like sleeping in your own bed. It was bitter sweet saying goodbye to our wonderful nurses, I went out to get them some little nibbles and a thank you card. As a nurse, I know how nice it is when we get thank you messages from our patients. The one thing they asked us to do was to go back to them when we were all done with treatment and everything else. At this point we didn't know what lay ahead. Below are a few pointers on how to deal with having a loved one in the hospital.

1. The goal of the medical team is to get your loved one better and they are there as your support, work with them so you can have a conducive relationship with them. They usually have a full workload on their plate as well so be respectful and they will be respectful back to you.
2. If you are planning on staying in the hospital to provide support for your loved one bring some comfortable clothes and things to keep you busy.
3. Have some bottled water and healthy snacks for the times when the cafeteria is closed.
4. As a caretaker staying in the hospital you should be mindful of your own needs. Dealing with the reality of what is going on can suddenly hit you when you least expect it take the time to speak to someone before it becomes too much to handle.
5. The hospital social workers are a great help they can be a great resource to ask questions about all the different things you might be worried about such as work or finances. They are also a good resource for giving you coping mechanisms.
6. Don't be shy to ask for help when it is being offered, you are not a super human being and it is okay to ask for help. Most people are willing to do the little things for you because they love you and they want to be there for you.
7. Take the time to do some self-care activities, even if it just means stepping out and going to sit out on a bench somewhere, you also need the time to process what is going on.

8 BIOPSY RESULTS

In all these steps, I am sure you are wondering what happened with the biopsy results. To refresh your memory the tumor was removed and the surgeon said a sample had been take so that it could be processed at the lab so that we could find out the type of tumor Tony had. Processing the biopsy usually takes 2 to 3 business days, since our surgery was on a Friday I wasn't really expecting it until the following Wednesday. We kept asking the rehab doctor and the results still were not in the chart. I didn't let this become the focus of my attention but it was difficult to ignore because most of our friends were so focused on finding out the results. To be honest I don't know what they thought knowing would do for them after all we were the ones that were going through this whole ordeal. I do understand there are people that like to know everything and you cannot fault them for that. As I grow older I have learned to realize that human beings are a unique species and we all come with our own perspective on life. In short people think and act differently, and as such there are those that like to have some control by having certain information. Just because I don't function like that does not necessarily mean it is wrong.

Back to the topic at hand, we went home without knowing the actual results of the tumor, whether it was benign or malignant, and whether it would require further treatment. We had extensive discharge education and received a lot of printed information regarding what to expect after spinal surgery and a lot of it was overwhelming. Yes, I am a nurse but dealing with my patients is different to dealing with my personal situation. There is a professional distance you develop as part of self-perseverance, to give my patients a 100% I must keep some distance so that I don't break down mid shift. That's not to say there aren't situations where that protective barrier cracks and I end up having an emotional break. There are situations that are just sad and depressing and no amount of professional distance can protect you from those. In my husband's case, it was personal and close to home this was the guy I had promised to love in sickness and in health but never imagined the sickness would come this soon. After all we were finally getting along now (side joke). But seriously this illness and surgery took us by surprise.

So where was I, discharge training. We had a follow up plan to follow up with our primary care physician (my hero doctor), our surgeon (young and high tech), the oncologist and the radiation oncologist. We were also expected to continue outpatient physical therapy as recommended by the rehab doctor. We knew that recovery would be long. Thankfully I had time off from work thanks to living in a State like California. I could benefit from paid family leave while my job was protected. Those that are against such programs obviously haven't had the unexpected happen to them. I am thankful I could take the time out to be available for all that my husband has been going through. Having the surgery was just the beginning of the journey, the healing and recovery process happens over time.

We are continuing with treatment and follow up. Back to the tumor results. The first appointment we had after being discharged home was with our surgeon. As you know we left rehab without knowing what the pathology results were. We went to the surgery follow up appointment expecting to get the results we had been anxiously waiting for, we were not the only ones waiting for the results our friends and family members were also understandably concerned. The appointment generally went well, he was excited by the progress that Tony was making and he was also happy with the way the wound was healing. When it came to pathology results we were informed that the biopsy sample had been sent to the Mayo clinic for further analysis as the local hospital had been unable to identify the type of tumor it was. How much stranger could things get, we remained thankful for all that had been done for Tony but we still needed some sort of closure because at this point the tumor was still a mystery. We were assured that we would be contacted directly by phone as soon as he received the results, as it was the treatment plan was still not very clear. What we knew for sure was that most of the tumor was safely removed but since there had been no clear boundary between the tumor and the spinal cord the surgeon had left bits of the tumor in place. The treatment plan would then depend on the tumor type, we were told that we would most probably need radiation as the best treatment option but this would depend on the tumor type. We knew to expect to see the radiation oncologist again but this would have to be after the results. We were told to book a follow up appointment for a months' time.

We had a follow up appointment with our primary care physician as well. This was like a great reunion, I don't know whether I have made it clear at all but this doctor is a ROCK STAR. It is all thanks to him that Tony got the surgery he needed. He is a real-life hero personified, he goes to all lengths for his patients and I thank God for giving my husband the foresight that made him select him as his primary care physician. Seeing doctor Hero again was great I could personally thank him for his dedication in going all out for my husband, he was the one that pushed for him to get seen by the other specialists on that fateful day that his blood pressure was still super high despite having been on blood pressure medication for a week. It was now time to get a feel of what had happened and where we went from here. Tony was using a walker and he was in a lot of pain so doctor Hero's focus at this point was to make sure that Tony's pain was well managed.

Well the pain thing also ended up becoming a cause of some drama, have you had to deal with the insurance companies regarding pain control. Well here is what happened - doctor Hero on examining my husband figured out that the blood pressure was still high and a contributing factor was the pain. He reviewed the pain regiment he was currently on and decided to order some Oxycontin every 12 hours and then to have the option of Percocet for breakthrough pain. The idea was to limit the number of pills he was taking because he would be getting the long acting pain medication. This sounded like a great idea because he was going to be needing good pain control for physical therapy. Well we left with our prescription and went to the pharmacy we had to leave it and they told us they would let us know once the medication was ready. The prescription never got ready, in fact it was declined by the insurance company and that woke the angry woman in me.

We received a letter from the insurance company notifying us that the prescription for oxycontin had been declined because it did not meet medical necessity. There was criteria that they felt had to be met before a prescription for OxyContin could be prescribed. For starters, they wanted him to have tried different pain medication and then fail on that medication before they would approve the stronger pain medication. This made no sense to me, I know there are people that can potentially abuse pain medication but at this point my husband did not meet this. This was a guy who was in acute pain because of major spinal surgery. He was in constant pain and needed his pain to be well controlled so that he could tolerate physical therapy, how much simpler could it be. I was not happy about the decision and I decided to put in a complaint. I called the insurance company and got to express my frustration. We were already close to finishing the pain medication that had been prescribed from rehab and he needed something to help with the pain as he went through continued rehab. So there I was spending my day arguing with the insurance company. The decision had been made by their medical reviewer, my question was, how does someone who hasn't even physically assessed the patient decide the best treatment course? I wanted to speak to this person or at minimum I wanted access to the research base that they use to come up with these blanket policies. I let my distress be known, I would not give up until my concerns were heard. The lady I spoke to was helpful. She worked with the doctor's office to get the pain prescription changed to something that they would approve. This was not the outcome I wanted but it was the next best thing.

I was not going to let it rest because I did not agree with their policy. The term medical necessity just rode me up the wrong way. To me it means they (the insurance company) has an idea of what medical necessity is and they use their criteria to decide whether to approve treatment based on what they deem medical necessity. The reason I didn't like this is because there can be some unique situations that do not fit into their little boxes and these should be treated on a case by case basis and because of that I decided to put in an official complaint through the department of health. I have enclosed a portion of the letter I sent for clarity

Having recently been diagnosed with a spinal tumor my husband had spinal surgery for removal of said tumor on September 23rd, following which he stayed 2 days in ICU, 1 day in a step-down unit and 4 days in an Acute Rehab unit. He has been having ongoing pain not responsive to his discharge prescription of Percocet 5/325. He still requires physical therapy as he is nowhere close to functioning at his pre-surgery level. I am taking time off work to help care for him and he struggles with daily activities and pain is one of the limiting factors. His primary care physician recommended starting him on Oxycontin 10 mg, the health plan has denied him coverage due to LACK of MEDICAL NECESSITY. They recommend a trial of MS Contin. I am concerned about the process they use to determine medical necessity

1. How do they to determine what medical necessity is?

2. No one from the health plan called or contacted us to assess how my husband's pain was affecting his daily living situation.

3. His physician prescribed the medication based on his physical assessment of my husband's condition, how does someone who is in an office somewhere feel he is the best person to judge medical necessity based on a review of a chart and not the actual patient.

4. My husband's pain is acute requiring acute treatment to continue with physical therapy and healing, trialing other medications first delays his healing.

5. I was not given sufficient explanation to explain the denial of the coverage, their jargon should not be made to apply to every patient because every situation is different.

6. I would like access to the research and rationale they have used to make such determinations because it clearly isn't for the patient's benefit.

7. Is the decision based on a bias that we are not aware of.

8. We pay insurance premiums for a reason, and to be denied coverage for a reason that seems ridiculous is a slap in the face

9. Do they communicate with physicians regarding what medical necessity is, I mean why would a physician with over 30 years of experience in the medical field prescribe medication if he felt it was not medically necessary

10. Pain is what he patient says it is, my husband has never abused pain medication in is life and I can't fathom why a Medical Reviewer (who is a Physician) would deny to approve him pain medication based on a blanket policy.

I did receive a call from the department of health and they are following up on the complaint. Even though my husband did get another prescription I did not withdrawal my complaint because I don't want the next person to be denied needed pain medication based on some vague blanket policy.

9 THE LONG ROAD TO RECOVERY

Tony started physical therapy a few weeks after being discharged from rehab and we were getting used to being at home and taking each day as it came. We did get the phone call from the neurosurgeon who was pleased to inform us that the tumor had finally been identified as a pilocytic astrocytoma. If you are to get a tumor I guess this is the type to get, I say this because it is considered a low-grade tumor and it usually stays in the areas where it starts and it is also considered benign. Pilocytic astrocytoma's generally form sacs of fluid or may be enclosed within a cyst, although they are usually slow growing these tumors can become very large. In the case of my husband we have no idea how long he had the tumor for, but we do know that it had grown very large and that is why it had started causing all those symptoms.

Having heard the results the surgeon reassured us that based on the type of tumor it was we might not need further treatment but we still had to follow up with the radiation oncologist. When we called to make an appointment with the radiation oncologist we were told that he wanted to have the PET scan results available. Before the emergency surgery we had been scheduled to get a PET scan done, it was believed that the PET scan would have been able to identify abnormal cells and therefore assist in the diagnosis. We could schedule the PET scan and then follow up with the radiation doc, who I will now refer to as doctor Radiation from here on out.

We went to see doctor Radiation and he went over the PET Scan results, which were generally okay apart from an abnormality within the head/neck area which he was going to get a referral to an Ear, nose and throat specialist to have a look at. In the meantime, we were informed that Tony's case was discussed at the Tumor Board, apparently, there is a tumor board that consists of different specialists from the main cancer specialty hospitals within the local area. Specialist doctors meet to discuss different cases to come up with the best treatment plan based on current research and recommendations. We later learned that Doctor Hero had pushed for Tony's case to be discussed at the tumor board. So, this group of doctors from all the oncology specialist hospitals met up to discuss his case. Based on the recommendations from everyone it was agreed that he would benefit from radiation therapy. A repeat MRI was going to be needed to help in tailoring the treatment plan. We also had to go in for an appointment with the treatment team for a citing session.

With all the radiation preparation going on we also had to see the ENT specialist. He was very nice and was just amazed to hear about Tony's story. To have all this happen at the age of 40 is rather shocking and kind of a big deal. We have chosen to focus on the positive because it can be so easy to get stuck feeling sorry for ourselves. He considered his nasal passage and found a deviated septum and wait for it, A MASS. Again, I decided to look at the positive, which to me was that at least we had found something that could be acted upon. Imagine never knowing and never being able to do anything about it. The assessment also found that Tony had an area of swelling around his left neck area. To further diagnose and figure out a treatment plan DR ENT felt that an MRI was warranted. In my practical mind, I felt we could try and get the outstanding MRIs done at the same time. If you recall he needed an MRI to help with the radiation and now he needed an orbital MRI to figure out what the mass was. We left the appointment with a plan to arrange an appointment once the MRI was done. With all that has been going on I remain thankful for the health insurance we have, pain medication issues aside.

We made the booking and at first the MRI center could fit in the appointments for the same day. This was great because it was going to save multiple drives. This excitement was short lived we received a call the following day telling us that they could not do both MRIS on the same day. We therefore rescheduled one of them for a different day. The radiation schedule was dependent on the results of the spinal MRI as this is what the doctor was planning on using to help guide the therapy. The orbital MRI was completed and all hubby had to do was wait and hear on those results

The day after the MRI we were called by DR ENTs office to ask hubby to go in to discuss the results. I mentioned earlier on that getting called into the Doctors office to hear results usually means something is up and in this case it was. The Doctor called in to go over the results and go over a treatment plan. There was a mass that he planned on removing and the lump by the side of the neck was lymph node that he was going to biopsy, added to that he also planned to fix the deviated septum. All these were planned to be done on the same day as outpatient procedures. Added to these we still had to deal with radiation once it started. With all this going on its easy to get into victim mode because you do sit and wonder when will it all stop.

However, as I have said before I have decided to have a different outlook on life by choosing faith. That is the reason I have decided to write this book. In sharing our story, I aim to offer some hope to those that are going through similar situations. When things are not going our way or when the worst seems to be happening it is so easy to get lost in our own misery but I want to share is that we can use such times as opportunities for growth. I am therefore sharing the lessons that I have taken from my own personal experience, I am taking it all as an opportunity for continued growth. We also decided as a family to take this as an opportunity to improve our health as a family while showing

Tony support. He still had high blood pressure and he was placed on a strict low salt cardiac diet.

1. Get the family involved in any health improvement plans that you may have. There is nothing worse than feeling like the odd man out.
2. Take walks outside to get some fresh air and gentle exercise.
3. Increase your intake of water, fruits, and vegetables.
4. Get in the habit of reading food labels, you will be surprised how much salt is in the foods we eat.

10 THE RADIATION PROCESS

After the MRI was done and the Doctor had the opportunity to look over the scans to tailor the radiation therapy. We had to go in for a citing visit. This is where they had Tony lying on the radiation table while they use the radiation machine which kind of looks like another MRI machine. They had him lay there so they could mark him and figure out the best position for him to lie on for the radiation rays to specifically target the remainder of the tumor. It was interesting to see how the machine works and the team did such a good job at explaining what to expect, and just like that we were ready to get going.

Tony started the radiation in mid-December, we were warned that it can cause fatigue. At this point I had gone back to work as my 6 weeks paid family leave was up. Work was flexible enough to let me work the days I could. I opted to mainly work weekends so that I could be available for transporting him back and forth from appointments. He ended up needing 5 weeks' worth of radiation. The way radiation works is that the Doctor decides how much radiation you need and then that dose is divided into smaller doses to be given daily over short spans of time to limit the length of time that one is exposed to radiation.

I was there for the first radiation and the actual therapy didn't take long. It was given over a 15-minute period and apparently didn't hurt. Per Tony it just felt a little uncomfortable. We had also been informed that it could eventually cause a burning sensation in the throat. So, over the length of the radiation there were some days I could not make it with him and on the days I could I was there with him. In between everything we had been back to the surgeon who had said that Tony could progress to drive as tolerated. This was helpful because it allowed him to drive himself to some of the sessions. Added to that he also had a lot of procedures to contend with.

He had the nasal mass removed as an outpatient appointment and we are thankful to report that it was just a mass with no cancer cells seen when they did the biopsy. He also required a fine needle aspiration of the left neck lymph node to test for cancer. Doctor Hero wasn't keen on this, he said that based on his experience this type of test is never a good one for identifying anything and he bet a $100 that the results would be inconclusive. Disclaimer …. he did not bet in the literal sense. To his credit that is exactly what ended up happening. The result came back saying the quality of the sample was not ideal and cancer could not be confirmed or ruled out. Not very useful results to guide any treatment or therapy. He was therefore referred to another surgeon to have a look at his lymph node with the possibility of having a lymphotomy. At this point we were becoming experts at receiving what most would consider bad news. We took it in our stride and waited for the appointment with Doctor Lymph Node... who is actually a highly-accomplished surgeon who also specializes in plastic surgery.

With so much going on it is easy to lose sight of the little things but we were there for the kids and it was also the Christmas time. This was where you learn that you have amazing people and support around you. We were playing catch up with the bills but we had decided no matter what the kids would get something for Christmas. We are so blessed and there is one wonderful awesome loving friend of ours who took it upon herself to shop for our kids. Her son and our oldest have been friends since they were in 4th grade and we have been in a car pool for years. She has become family and she took on all the driving while all this has been going on. She did it out of the kindness of her heart and doesn't even want to be credited for anything. She took the time to go and shop for our kids and I mean literally shop, she bought them practical clothes that they will be able to grow into. She put a thought into each article of clothing that she bought. I have been so humbled by what this woman has done that I have no words to express my gratitude. I believe God brought her into our life for a special reason and that was to show us that he is out there and he has his angles here looking out for us. Thanks to her my kids had a wonderful Christmas and I will forever be indebted to her for her kindness and love. She said she was just doing something that others have already done for her. That concept of paying it forward is real. I also hope to be able to do something similar for someone soon.

Radiation went on until after Christmas and ended in the 3rd week of January. In terms of the lymph node Tony decided to go for another procedure that they can use instead of surgery. As you may or may not know when consenting patients for procedures the surgeon must go over all the possible things that can happen and this list seemed intense for Tony considering we didn't even know whether there was any cancer involved. Spinal surgery has more intense things that could go wrong but we opted for that surgery because of all the symptoms he was experiencing at that time. By questioning whether there was another option for diagnosing before proceeding with surgery we found out that there was another procedure that could be done. It is called a core needle biopsy; this procedure takes more of a sample than the fine needle biopsy.

This again was an outpatient procedure meaning Tony didn't have to stay overnight. I was already scheduled to work the night before the procedure but thankfully I had the day off to be able to pick him up and be there for the end of the procedure. They thought they would have to give him some light sedation so our plan was for me to pick him up after my shift as his procedure was scheduled for the morning. After work I drove myself to the hospital he was having the procedure at. As I was driving in to find parking, Tony called me to let me know that his procedure was done and he didn't need to be driven as they had not given him any sedation therefore he could drive himself. Since I had already planned on staying over after my shift we opted to stop by our very good friends house where I took a shower, ate, relaxed, and got social for a while before driving back home. I am happy to report that weeks later we found out that the biopsy was negative and that was another blessing for us. Imagine if we had opted for the initial surgery that was being recommended. Since we did have an out-patient procedure I have decided to include a few pointers on what you can do to prepare for an out -patient procedure.

1. Try and book your procedure on a day that works well for you.
2. If you must have sedation you will need to have someone to take you home as you will not be able to drive yourself.
3. You must consider making alternative arrangements for childcare especially if your significant other is the one that will be the one to pick you up.
4. Ask all the relevant questions prior to your scheduled date so that you can be psychologically prepared for what to expect.
5. Follow the pre-procedure instructions that you are given, this usually includes not eating and drinking the night before your procedure.
6. Work considerations have to be taken into account, sick day for yourself as well as for your significant other especially if they are going to be the one to pick you up.

11 POWER OVER MIND

You control how you respond to a situation. The biggest lesson that I would like to share is that you have the power over your mind. What you choose to focus on is in your hands. Learning this small lesson has been my saving grace these past few years. I am blessed to have an amazing friend who paid for me to attend Tony Robbins's " Unleash the Power Within" two years ago. Through Tony's teachings I have learned that what we focus on is what we get. If I had chosen to focus on the negatives when I heard about my husband's tumor you can imagine what that would have done to my mood and my general outlook on life. It is easy to get into victim mode and that is the fastest way to feeling sorry for yourself. It could have been so easy to start the why questions, why me, why now, what have we done to deserve this. But just as it is so easy to fall into that kind of thinking it is just as easy to think differently. That's right in the darkness there is always some light. You may ask what light is there in finding out that your spouse has a spinal tumor. In my case I found plenty. I saw the miracle that God had worked in our life and I chose to believe that Gods hand guided all that had happened. Follow me if you will, my husband had been under the care of a different Doctor before he transferred to doctor Hero. In the time he was seen by the other doctor he had complained of back pain but the assessment and treatment had stopped at x rays and physical therapy. An MRI was required to identify his tumor.

By some unexplainable action, he switched doctors and just happened to select a primary care physician who just happened to have extensive background in radiation medicine. Call it coincidence if you may but I choose to see that as God working in our favor, because of that I chose to look at the positive in the given situation. Yes, hubby had a tumor but at least we found out about it and something could be done about it. See just by focusing my mind on what the positives were in the situation I was able to cope and avoid going into victim mode. Although this is not always easy, I mean let's face it there are some sucky things that happen in this life and I am sure the last thing you want to hear when you see that your world is crumbling down is to look at the positive side of a given situation. I would like you to try and do this the next time you have something bad happen to you. It won't always be easy but it will give you a different perspective on life. It literally will lift a load, there is nothing worse than the stress of constant worry that focusing on the negative can bring. Changing your focus can help guide you in a productive light.

When you find yourself getting overwhelmed by your current situation I would like you to consider doing the following things

1. Stop and take a deep breath, let your mind focus on the now. Re align your thoughts by just focusing on the now. Appreciate what you have in front of you. Let your mind focus on your breathing, close your eyes as you breath in if that helps. That action can help slow down your thought process .
2. Be thankful, give thanks for what you have in that given situation. Yes you might be going through something in the moment but I am sure you have some things to be thankful for as well. Your family, your health, your friends, your career, your opportunities. The list is endless there is always something we can be thankful for.

In taking a moment in time to focus on something other than your problems you give your brain the chance to refocus its energy. Take your problems as an opportunity for growth. As much as it might be overwhelming in the moment know that your situation will pass and you can use your problems to guide you to a better future. That is exactly what I decided to do with what we were dealt. The problem was there and it could not be taken away so the only option left to us was to deal with it. Like I said it could have been so easy to focus on the tumor, the problem with that is that it would have made me stuck. My brain would have been stuck focusing on the problem so instead I decided to focus on the good in the given situation. The good in our situation was we have a great doctor who has proven himself to be a great patient advocate with the bonus of being a specialist in radiation oncology. We had a treatment plan and so far everything has been good. Yes it is a minor setback in our life goals but at the same time we have used the situation as a wakeup call.

We become stagnant, we make plans but never work on them. This situation has made us realize that life is unpredictable and that we have to learn to live in the present. We have learned to enjoy the time we have with our family. Focusing on what we don't have or how horrible our lives are only makes us live ungrateful lives. We really do have the power to choose the life we want to live. This is the simplest advice I can offer anyone, for the longest time I let situations dedicate my outlook on life. The biggest aha moment in my life was when I made the realization that only I had the power to control how I responded to given circumstances. I may not have had control over the situations but I certainly had the control over how I chose to respond to what may have appeared like the end of the world in that given situation. Do I allow it to ruin my day and mood by letting the situation overwhelm my focus. It certainly is easy to blame life, circumstances etc. but how far is focusing on blame going to get you. As my mama would say in any given situation you must pick yourself up dust off the dirt and move on to a better tomorrow and key to this is the realization that only you have the power to make that decision to move on.

Choosing to get stuck in your unpleasant situation only delays you getting the better tomorrow that is coming to you. Learn from the situation and use it as a bouncing board to your better tomorrow. That is exactly what my hubby and I have decided to do with the cards that we have been dealt. We have decided to use it as a the eye opener that it is. Life is not guaranteed we have to make the most of the life we have today. We do not want to live our life in regrets. I recently read the book "Life's Golden Ticket" by Brendon Burchard and three questions he asks are did you live?, did you love?, and did you matter?. I have found these three questions keep playing in my mind and I have decided to make an effective movement towards doing things that matter. I want to love, I want to live, and I want to matter. The beginning of that is by being grateful for this second chance we have at life. I have never felt more alive and I want to use this platform to encourage others to start living their best lives now. Stop focusing on the what could have been and start focusing on what could be.

For us that is grabbing our issues by the horns and going full throttle at creating the life that we want to live on our terms. We have no shortage of dreams, every year we start with a list of things we want. More time with family, financial freedom, reduction in debt, family vacations , more date nights, and the list is endless. However nothing changes as we go back to accepting the status quo. After al,l society says if you have a job you should be grateful right. Well I have realized that there is nothing wrong with wanting more and that when you have more you are better able to help your fellow man. So after this situation I give myself and my family permission to want and work for more. That starts with the acknowledgement that we have a lot of work ahead of us and the beginning of that is acknowledging there is a problem that stops the fulfilment of our goals.

To me that has been the acknowledgment that we have a problem with debt. This acknowledgement has been freeing because I believe it is the beginning of better things to come. Once we get our debt situation under control we can have the type of life we want but there is no point putting everything off we can start today.

I therefore decided to start planning and taking action towards improving our financial picture, the common denominator is the knowledge and continued realization that I am the only person that can change my current situation and that goes back to what I have been saying in this chapter. Only you have the control over your mind and how you decide to respond to the challenges and opportunities you face in your day to day existence.

Our current situation has been a blessing in that it has made us realize that we need to have a better financial picture.

12 THE FINANCIAL PICTURE

If you recall from the beginning of this book I said that I was grateful for the fact that I live in California. I got time off to be at home to care for my husband and received a percentage of my regular pay. This was a blessing because realistically speaking our finances would not have been able to handle my being at home without having that regular paycheck coming in. We have literally become slaves to our current situation. We work to pay our bills yet when we need time off to care for a loved one we can't afford to take the time off from work because of how our finances are set up. I am here to try and get people to open their eyes to their current financial situation and work towards fixing it. There seems to be a guilt factor associated with talking about money. We need to start treating money as a tool that can be used to fulfill our dreams. There is nothing wrong with dreaming big but we must realize that we must be able to plan and prepare for those times when our income generation ability is taken away from us. In this case, ask yourself whether you are prepared for what would happen if you are physically unable to work for that paycheck that you have become so reliant on?. It took our current experience for me to realize that we are far from prepared. I learned that having an emergency fund should be treated as a financial priority. I used to ask how can I be expected to save for an emergency fund when I can't even make a dent in my current student loan debt. My thinking has now changed, by not having an emergency fund we are opening the opportunity for us to dig ourselves into a financial hole that will be extremely difficult to climb out of.

I took paid family leave from the state of California but that only lasted 6 weeks, if we had a sufficient emergency fund I would have been able to stay at home a bit longer and be there to support my husband through the radiation that he had to have but since the bills don't stop just because you are not working the common-sense action for me to take was to go back to work.

Again, I can choose how I respond to our financial situation in 2 ways. I can feel sorry for us and be stuck in pity, this will drain my energy and keep me stuck in this financial mess. I can acknowledge we have a problem and choose to do something about it. There is no hero waiting to come and save me. I must be the hero of my own story.

Choosing option 2, I am on a road to financial freedom and I am making sure that my family is on board as well. I like to believe that if we had not gone through what we have had to go through this last quarter of 2016 we would have continued to live in the false reality we were living in. That is accepting the status quo being stuck in employment with no proper exit strategy in place after all we had the so-called security of receiving a paycheck every 2 weeks. That outlook has now changed, yes, it's great to have a paycheck and secure job but every so often check back to see where you are in terms of achieving your goals. I encourage you to take a serious look at where your life is right now and whether this is the life you dreamed of living. If it is then I am truly happy for you. If it is not, then perhaps now is the time to start planning the steps you need to take to get it to where you want it to be.

There is no short cut to success and success requires a lot of hard work but it all starts with a decision and small action steps. What works for me in keeping my focus is the constant feeding of my mind. Reading has been my saving grace, I seek out wisdom and inspiration from those that have gone before me. There are a lot of successful people out there that are more than willing to share their lessons. When you seek answers, you begin to find them. I have been reading a lot on budgeting and money management and although I currently consider myself a novice it won't take me long to move through the stages and finally become an expert. Knowing that I am not exactly a novice, I do know some basic financial principles but I just haven't applied them consistently. Today is the day I choose to change how I approach my finances. I have gone ahead and started seeking out information on budgeting and I am ready to take on this next challenge. The biggest step has been taken, and that is the acknowledgement that there is work to be done. It's kind of like admitting to being an addict and now taking the steps to recover. Although daunting I am excited by the journey I have started on I can't wait to get to financial freedom. I am excited by the vision I have for my life and although it took a major life event to get me there I am grateful for the opportunity to change our family's financial future. I am also taking it as an opportunity to teach those that are willing to learn, that the better tomorrow you dream of can only happen if you decide to take the steps required to change your circumstances. Just as you feed yourself when you are hungry, you must also take the action to change your situation.

What I have discovered about my spending habits is that I just spend without thinking through the purchases. I know we make good money and we should have a healthy savings cushion but there is something to be said about instant gratification. I think most of us suffer from it. One thing I have learned and that I will now start taking seriously is the concept of savings. I do put aside money every month but because I have easy access to it I find myself dipping in and depleting the savings and then having to start from scratch. To change this I am changing my accessibility to our savings. I am changing the destination of our savings from my day to day account to an online only savings account. It takes 3-5 business days to get money out of this type of bank account therefore reducing the temptation to always dip into the account. My goal is to grow our savings to a cushion of about $20,000, that is nowhere close to what we really need to have as an emergency fund but we must start somewhere. Peace of mind will go a long way to keeping us motivated to continue working on our financial goals. It will also be so much easier to give back to society.

We are also going to work hard at paying off our debt and I know for sure we will have no credit card debt and one less car loan by the end of this year. Writing down our debt was rather revealing. It made us realize we had a lot of debt but at the same time it also made us realize that if we plan and stick to it we can greatly reduce the amount of debt we have. Our biggest debts are our student loans and we do have a plan for those as well. We know that trying to pay off our student loans based on our current income alone is not going to cut it as that will take forever, we therefore need to increase our income streams, that's where the concept of multiple income streams comes in. Due to a desire to be financially independent we figure out the best way of doing this is to consider entrepreneurship. We are therefore both working on our respective businesses, mine is a clothing line and his is a virtual reality/rendering business. It's very unlikely that hubby will be able to go back to his job because it requires a long commute and his back muscles won't be able to handle that. So rather than waiting for the day his disability ends we have decided to be proactive in planning for that eventuality. We have been putting in the work and are excited about launching the business soon. We are sending good vibes into the rest of 2017, yes 2016 was tough especially towards the end but the way we look at it 2017 can only get better

There is a lot to be said to having an optimistic outlook on life, it keeps you grateful for what you have. Let's be real, the last couple of months haven't been a walk in the park but I can assure you we have it better than other people in this world out there.

13 THE STORY CONTINUES

We are in September of 2017 and a lot has been happening in terms of Tony's recovery process and life in general. I had hoped I would be done with writing this book but our story continues. Tony is still at home and the business is still not launched. We are still dealing with doctor's appointments and pain issues. He has continued to experience pain and the medication he was taking was just making him sleepy. He has followed up with both the radiation MD and the neurosurgeon and they all seem to think the pain could be a result of the nerve damage that might have occurred as a result of the radiation treatment. Apparently this is rather common, he has therefore had his medication changed around a bit. He also had a repeat MRI scan which showed that the tumor was still there but this is expected as the surgeon did say he had removed what he could safely remove without the risk of causing some major long-term damage. It now appears that Tony might be dealing with some long term pain issues so we are officially joining the chronic back pain crew . We have been looking at alternatives and have been hearing good things about acupuncture. We delayed this as we wanted to make sure that all the Doctors would be supportive. I am a nurse but am not a back specialist we wanted to make sure that the acupuncture would in no way be contraindicated based on the surgery Tony has had. We have been okayed by the doctors but now we are waiting for insurance approval and that is taking forever to sort out.

We may have to actually pay out of pocket as it is coming to over a month.

Speaking of insurance, I must share the frustration that you should expect to deal with when dealing with employer sponsored long term disability claims. Since Tony has been out of work on disability pay for over 3 months he qualified to apply for the long-term disability supplement that his employer offers. Honestly speaking I had never paid much attention to the different benefits that we get from our employers but now I have started. Experience is truly a great teacher. My venting is based on our personal experience and I am in no way saying this is how most insurance companies work but our experience has been less than stellar.

One thing I can share is that getting set up and signed on to insurance is easy, after all they are a business and they want your business. However, what I am learning in dealing with most insurance companies in terms of filing a claim and getting the claim paid out is not as easy.

Tony has long term insurance through his employers and the human resources rep for his employer did forward us the papers to claim the long-term disability from his policy. Little did we know it would be like trying to qualify for the Olympics. The process is tedious. I am convinced they make it this way as a means of burning you out so that you just give up and let it go. Disclaimer – these opinions are mine based on what I have seen my husband have to go through in order to get the long term disability payments

So first of what is long term disability especially as it relates to us. In our case being out of work for over three months qualifies Tony to claim long term disability payments through his employer sponsored long term disability plan. The idea is to have his pay supplemented while he is out on disability. He Currently gets a disability check from the state of California and this about 60% of his actual Salary. The Long-term disability is meant to supplement his disability checks to bring his payments as close to his regular pay as much as possible. As you can imagine this is a great resource to have. It hasn't been easy dealing with the insurance company but I am pleased to report they finally approved his claim and we are now receiving the payments. Tony's ordeal has made me reassess my own benefit coverage and I am also going to get myself signed up for critical care insurance, after all we have learned that life happens. The best gift we can give our families is to be prepared for the unimaginable.

As I continue to write Tony continues on his road to recovery. A recent MRI showed some fluid collection around the tumor area. This might explain the pain and blood pressure issues he has been experiencing. A 2 month follow up MRI has been requested so that the neurosurgeon can better reassess his condition. If the repeat MRI ends up showing a change in the fluid collection then he might have to have some sort of procedure if needed. We therefore remain grateful that we have the insurance coverage that allows for this continuous follow up.

While all that is going on we made the huge decision to travel to Africa so that I can meet the side of his family that I haven't had the opportunity to meet. The kids were overly excited about travelling as they got the opportunity to spend time with cousins and appreciate their culture. Tony and the kids travelled before me and I joined them for the last 2 weeks of the vacation. I am thankful to have had the opportunity to travel and one thing we made sure of was to purchase travel insurance. Hero doctor wasn't overly excited about letting Tony travel but he made sure to drill into us the need to make arrangements for him to travel back at the earliest signs of any symptoms. We will continue to appreciate all the advantages we have and make the most of every minute we have on this precious world. We are back to the swing of things and as the 1 year anniversary of his surgery approaches I am busy scrambling to get this book proofed and published by the 23rd of September. This is my first book and I hope it will not be the last. Our spinal journey continues the repeat MRI has been done and we are waiting to hear whether the fluid collection around the spine is still there and whether there is going to be need for a procedure to drain it.

I am learning that this journey is ongoing so I will still go ahead and publish the book as planned. I will provide any updates through social media as I plan on being very open and transparent as it appears this journey is not yet over

I hope this book and our experience has somehow offered some great lessons learned and that it has made you start thinking about your life, your goals, and your future. If you can take anything from this book today it is my hope that you will stop, take a breath, and reassess your life.

Is now the time to revisit your life's goals?

ABOUT THE AUTHOR

Doctor Fatsani Dogani is a loving wife and mother of 3. She is originally from Malawi but considers herself a global citizen as she has had the opportunity to live in different countries and currently resides in California, USA. An avid reader and academic Fatsani is a nurse and PhD holder. She is also an entrepreneur who has recently partnered in an online clothing store that aims to contribute to improving the livelihoods of African artisans. Her recent experience with her husband's illness has awakened her long term goal of becoming an author. She hopes this is the first of many books to come.

www.ingramcontent.com/pod-product-compliance
Lightning Source LLC
Chambersburg PA
CBHW071634040426
42452CB00009B/1622